Table of Content

Editorial

Welcome to Rotterdam!

Rotterdam is not „just a city" in the Netherlands.
It is the most important port of Europe. A paradise of architecture, art, and enjoyment of life. See Skyscrapers and unusual buildings.

This guide has been written for visitors of the city. It contains a great route through the city center with it's most important attractions. The route is easy to understand and allows you to explore the city on your own.

I love Rotterdam. When I speak to a stranger, I often hear „Rotterdam? Is this a city I should visit.?" – and I definitely have to say: Yes! I have written this guide as I want to show tourists the most beautiful places of this city.

With my guide, it should be easy for you to discover the city totally on your own. But even if you have a problem, a question, or get lost, there is still help: Send me an e-mail and I will try to help you as soon as possible. See all details on the last page.

Map of Rotterdam: Downtown area

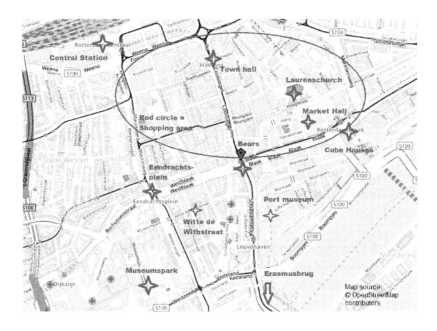

Map of Rotterdam: Kop van Zuid

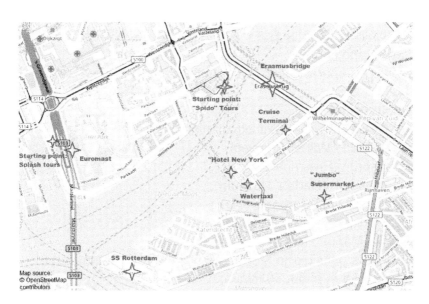

City tour: Introduction

The city tour is split into three durations:
You can choose to make the small tour, the medium tour, and the complete tour.
Of course, you can interrupt the tour and continue at another point, too: To make this guide fully flexible for you, the details how to reach the single attraction points, are mentioned.

Durations
Small tour: 3-4 approx. hours
Medium tour: 4-5 approx. hours
Complete tour: 6-7 approx. hours

The time you need for the tour depends on the time you take for the sightseeing points. The author strongly recommends taking care of the time carefully when you need to catch a train or anything else. The author does not bear any responsibility for mistakes.

The tour starts at the central point „Wilhelminapier", where the Cruise Terminal is located. When you didn't arrive by ship, take the metro lines C, D or E. Please look here for a short guide how to use the metro.
This route is separated into three parts:

Small city tour:
- Start: Cruise Terminal (Wilhelminapier)
- Kop van Zuid / Wilhelminaplein
- Erasmusbrug (Erasmus bridge)
- Havenmuseum (Harbor Museum)
- Oude Haven (Old Harbor)
- Kubuswoningen (Cube houses)
- Markthal (Market Hall)
- Meent (It is possible to stop the tour here and return to the starting point in about 30 minutes)

Medium city tour
(continuing the small city tour)
- Stadhuis (Town Hall)
- Schouwburgplein
- Rotterdam Centraal (Central Station Rotterdam)
- Westersingel
- Witte de Withstraat (It is possible to stop the tour here and
  return tot he starting point in about 20 minutes)

Complete city tour
(continuing the medium city tour)
- Museumpark (Park of Museums)
- Het Park (The Park)
- Euromast
- Veerhaven
  (End of tour. Return to the cruise center in about 15 minutes)

The city tour – small route

You start at the central point „Wilhelminaplein", which is located near the Erasmus Bridge (Erasmusbrug). When you follow this tour, you will walk over the bridge, so it is recommended that you go to the starting point by metro.

You can find a guide how to use the metro here.

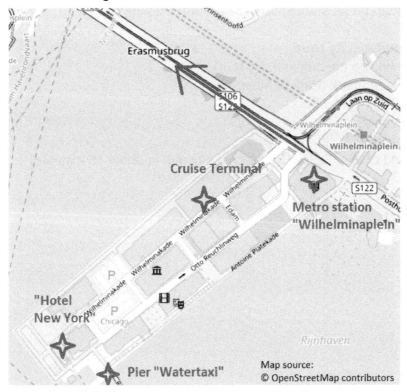

Map source:
© OpenStreetMap contributors

When you reach the station, follow the signs to Wilhelmina-pier and leave the station. Now, you already can see the huge Erasmusbridge and the water of the Rhine. When you keep your eyes in direction of the bridge, several attractions are located on the left side, and I recommend to take a look.

When you walk to the left side and take the right street called **Wilhelminakade,** you can reach the cruise terminal. During the summer month, every Thursday a large German cruise ship is laying here, but of course, some more cruise ships like the „Rotterdam" are going to Rotterdam. When there is a cruise ship docked in Rotterdam, it's a great idea to take some pictures from the Erasmusbridge. In the further part of this tour,

you will walk over the Erasmusbridge. Further behind the Cruise Termi- nal, at the foreland, is the famous **Hotel New York** located. Originally, it was the administration building of the **Holland-America Line**. Begin- ning its operation in 1873, the **HAL** transported many people from Europe migrated to the United States. Until 1925, about one million humans emigrated from the Nether- lands using the services of HAL.

Today, the beautifully renovated building contains the Hotel New York, which operates a good restaurant. All rooms in the building are looking like a ship. In the summer, a great terrace invites you to enjoy some typical Dutch snacks and an ice cold beer.

Attraction details:
Hotel New York
Location: Koninginnenhoofd 1, 3072 AD Rotterdam
Public transport: Metro D & E, Tram 23 & 25
www.hotelnewyork.nl

Only a few meter from the Hotel New York away, another attraction is waiting for you: The **Watertaxi**. There is a regular service to several points in the city center, but it's a real taxi service on the water, too: When you have the time and want to do, just walk inside of the office and ask them for a taxi service to the famous steamship „SS Rotterdam". Be careful: Don't forget to arrange the return journey with them.

Attraction details:
Watertaxi Rotterdam
Phone: +31 10 4030303
www.watertaxirotterdam.nl

Let's continue with the city tour. Walk the way back to the starting point and start your walk over the Erasmusbridge on the left side.

The Erasmusbridge (**Erasmusbrug**) was built in 1996 and is now the most important landmark for the city of Rotterdam. At this time, the area around the Wilhelminaplein, the so-called **Kop van Zuid**, was just an old harbor district, not in use anymore and full of descended houses. The Erasmus-bridge was the try to rebuild the district – with anenormous success, as you can see.

From the bridge, you can see the Cruise Terminal and the Hotel New York. On the other waterside the **Spido Tours**, the operator of harbor boat trips is located. A bit away you can see the observation tower Euromast. We will visit the tower in the last part of our complete city tour.

On the right side, you can see the red Willemsbridge and the defunct monument, the green rail bridge De Hef. It looks interesting from the distance, but it's not that interesting, so I can't recommend taking that way to the bridge.

Walk over the bridge, which will take about 15-20 minutes.

Once you have crossed the Erasmus Bridge, cross the large intersection and continue straight ahead. However, at the crossroads, you should change to the right side of the road. You are now entering the **Leuvehaven** area.

Right on the water, parallel to the main road (Schiedamse-dijk) is the harbor museum located. There are also some older boats in the water. If you follow the route through the Leuveha-ven, a seemingly provisional pontoon appears after about 500 meters, with which you can cross the anchorage. You will now reach the pretty street Wijnhaven.

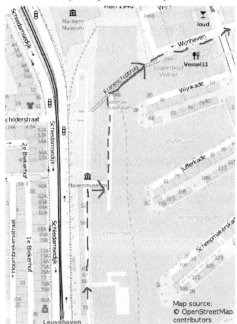

If the pontoon is blo-cked, take the Leuveha-ven straight ahead and then turn right into the main road Westblaak. After about 10 minutes' walk you will reach Blaak, that, you will see later anyways.

When you enter the street **Wijnhaven**, after about 500 meters you can see the white house (witte huis) on the left side, with the Westermeijer-sign on the rooftop. It was built in 1897 and was the tallest building in Europe. It has survived the Second World War as one of the few buildings in Rotterdam. It is grounded on about 1,000 wooden piles and is a protected monument.

Directly behind the Westermeijer-building, you can see the old port (Oudehaven). This is one of the oldest harbor parts of Rotterdam and built around 1350. Today, there are several nice cafes and the royal museum yard.

Turn left at the Oudehaven (into the street: Geldersekade). Now, you can already see the famous Cube houses. Go there upstairs to the inner courtyard.

In 1984, 51 cube houses were built in the center of Rotterdam. Nowadays, they are famous sights of the city. It is normal houses, but from the outside, it looks as though the walls are oblique in the interior.

In one of the houses is a small museum that gives you a feeling how to feel inside of a clubhouse. The museum is opened from 11.00 to 17.00 o' clock daily, the entrance fee is 3 Euro.

If you follow the inner courtyard of the Cube houses, you cross the large main road and get downstairs again on the other side. You are now in the central place *Blaak*.

Blaak is one of the most famous squares in the city. At this square is the church **Laurenskerk** located, as well as the new landmark of the city, the market hall (**Markthal**).

The Laurenskerk was built originally in 1449. In the 2nd world war, the church was heavily damaged during the bombardment of the German Luftwaffe on 14 May 1940, the church has been rebuilt until 1968.

When you see the market hall, the church looks almost tiny: The market hall opened in 2014 and is already a new sign of the city: It's the world's only market hall that contains market stalls, bars, restaurants, and apartments,  on the ceiling are huge paintings. The construction cost 175 million euro and has 11 floors. It is difficult to describe the flair of the market hall, so go and discover it on your own.

Attraction details:
Markthal Rotterdam
opened Monday - Friday from 10.00 to 20.00,
Saturday + Sunday from 12.00 to 18.00
Entrance: Free of charge.

When you pass the Markthal and the Laurenskerk, follow the way to the street Binnenrotte. After about 200 meters, turn left and walk into the street **Meent**.

When you pass the Markthal and the Laurenskerk, follow the way to the street Binnenrotte. After about 200 meters, turn left and walk into the street Meent.

Follow the street, and you will pass the Café Dudok, which is famous for the great apple pie (Appeltaart) with raisins and cinnamon.

Attraction details:
Café Dudok
Meent 88
Opening hours:
Monday-Thursday 08.00 – 23.00
Friday 08.00 – 01.00
Saturday 09.00 – 00.00
Sunday 09.00 – 23.00

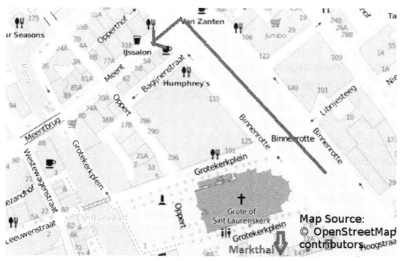

You have to follow the whole street Meent, for about 500 meters. Then, you will reach the main street *Coolsingel*. For your orientation: On the right side is a McDonald's restaurant in a glass-box-like building, the tram is riding on the main street.

The city tour – End of small route

End of small city tour:
If you want to stop here, just follow these instructions: The Coolsingel is the main street on which also the trams run - and from there you also come back quickly to the starting point, the **Wilhelminaplein**. Turn left into **Coolsingel**, then go straight.

You arrive at the **World Trade Center**, the **Beurs** Metro station, and finally the **Museumhaven** until you reach the **Erasmus Bridge**, which you only have to cross.

By the way, in the area between **Coolsingel** and **Beurs** are great possibilities for a shopping marathon: If you want to go shopping, feel free and explore the city.

If you don't want to walk anymore, follow the Coolsingel and you reach the metro station Beurs, which is a central interchange station. From here, you can take all available underground lines easily. Please see the instructions for using the metro, too.

16

The city tour – Medium route

Continue on the small city tour.
If you don't want to walk further, please see one page above for the way back to the starting point.

To proceed the tour, you just should have reached the main street **Coolsingel**. On the right side, you can see a McDonald's restaurant in a building, looking like a glass box. Turn right and pass the McDonald's restaurant.

After only a few meters, on the right side, you can see the town hall (Stadhuis). It was built between 1914 and 1920 and is one of the remaining buildings that didn't get destroyed in the second world war.

Cross the main street and follow the **Stadhuisplein**, so that you have the Stadhuis in the back and go away from it.

When you enter the Stadhuisplein, on the right, you can discover several restaurants: During the day, they offer normal food and drinks. But in the evenings, they transform into nightclubs and discotheques with entourage and entrance fees. Depending on the orientation of the respective venue, appropriate music is played here and you can celebrate your vacation all night.

Continue straight ahead, and after about 500 meters, you will finally reach the **Schouwburgplein**.

Schouwburg is the Dutch word for theater, so this is – translated into English - the theater square. Also, the theater of Rotterdam (**Rotterdamse Schouwburg**) is located here.

The original theater was destroyed in the Second World War - the current building was built in 1988. On the large square, next to water fountains are also some huge red lanterns, which can be moved freely with the controls you find on the square.

Picture source:
By Wikifrits (Own work) [CC BY-SA 3.0 (http:// creativecommons.org/ licenses/by-sa/3.0)], via Wikimedia Commons

Go straight ahead (on the left the Schouwburg, on the right the large square). You enter the alley *Mauritsplaats*, which flows into the *Mauritsweg*.

You pass a building that is a kind of special: The church of Paulus (*Pauluskerk*). In Rotterdam, a church is once again built, if it serves the particular architecture.

The Pauluschurch was opened in 2013 after the previous building (from the 1960iger-years, thus by no means of historical value) was demolished.

At the front, you see a beautiful green area with water in the middle. The water is a so - called water project.

When you look forward, you can see a beautiful park-like green space with water in the middle. This is the Westersingel. The water is the origin of the *Rotterdam Water project.*

The Water project was originally planned in 1841. At that time, the canals were mainly used for the supply and discharge of fresh water and sewage (!), as well as for drinking water. This naturally led to massive hygienic problems and cholera epidemics. That is why the government decided to create the Water project, which pumps fresh water from the river into the city.
In fact, the water quality was significantly improved, but there were still problems with cholera. From about 1870 the construction of the sewage system started.

Now, go to the right in direction of the central station (*Centraal Station*). A forecast advised a strong increase in passengers, so the government decided to rebuild the station totally. Nowadays, it is a further sign of architectural art, as the station is anything but „convenient".

From Rotterdam CS depart trains to the directions of Leeuwarden, Enschede, Venlo, The Hague, Utrecht, Amsterdam, Antwerp, and Brussels or Paris, to name just a few of the most important connections.

If you have seen enough, go the way back you came (*Westersingel & Mauritsweg*).

Follow the Westersingel for about 800 meters, and you will reach the Eendrachtsplein, where a metro station is located, too.

Here you can see the sculpture Santa Claus of the artist Paul McCarthy. Officially, the statue is showing Santa Claus holding a Christmas tree, but maybe you think it is looking like something else…?

And indeed: The unofficial name of the statue is **Kobold Buttplug (Kabouter Buttplug)**. When you take a look at the Dutch version of Wikipedia and enter **Buttplug**, you can see a picture of this sculpture…

Leave Kobold Buttplug alone and follow the Westersingel for more 250 meters.

Now, you have the choice:
This is the end of the medium city tour.

If you want to stop here, turn left into the **Witte de Withstraat**. This is a street of art and full of galleries. When you finished walking trough the Witte de Withstraat, turn right and you already can see the **Erasmusbridge**, where this tour started.

The city tour – Complete route

If you want to continue the tour, please continue reading here:

When you enter the road **Museumpark** from **Westersingel**, you will see the **Boijmans van Beuningen art museum** after a few meters.

It is easy to understand how the Museumpark came to his name, as there are no less than 6 museums and exhibitions in the immediate vicinity.

Follow the road for about 200 meters and turn left into the little **Melkkoppad**. It leads directly through the park. Take the time to relax and enjoy the park.

At the back end of the Museumpark, you will find the art gallery, as well as the Greek Orthodox Church, which is here since 1955.

Once you have crossed the Museumpark, you will reach a secondary road (separated only by a small dyke from the main road, the **Westzeedijk**.

From this point, you can already see the **Euromast**, still one of the tallest buildings in Rotterdam.

Walk right and under the tunnel of the art gallery. This part of the route is unfortunately not particularly attractive, but fortunately also not too long.

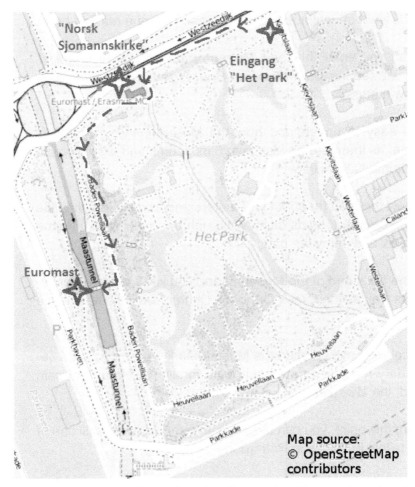

Map source:
© OpenStreetMap
contributors

Behind the tunnel, stairs lead up to the main street **Westzeedijk**. Take this, but follow the main road. After another 400 meters, you will see the tram stop **Kievitslaan**. Cross the street here and enter **Het Park** (translated simply: *The Park*).

The park is a nice connection to the **Euromast**, which is the next destination of our journey.

Unfortunately, there is no way to create an exact route for the park - so just go „for feeling" - you should always be able to see the tower.

If you do not want to go through the park, you can also follow the main road and take the second turn to the park at the Nordic sailor church.

Then follow the **Baden Powelllaan** secondary road, and you will come to a bridge that leads to the multi-lane main road to the Euromast.

VERY IMPORTANT: Do not use the multi-lane main road! It leads into the Maastunnel and is for automobiles only. Pedestrians may not use this tunnel! DANGER!

Welcome to the Euromast, with 185 meters one of the tallest buildings in Rotterdam. Built in 1960, it was originally „only" 101 meters high but then was increased in 1970 with the addition of the mast to 185 meters.

The Euromast can be visited, an elevator leads to the viewing platform at a height of 101m, where a restaurant is also housed. A rotating elevator, the so-called **Euroscope** brings you to the final height, which allows a fantastic view of city and harbor at good weather for up to 30km.

If you do not have high altitude, a visit to the Euromast is highly recommended.

Do you have land under your feet again?

Then it goes in the opposite direction: Into the earth. The next goal is the (almost) historic **Maastunnel**.

From the Euromast, head towards the water (the shore water is only a few meters away) and then turn left (in directiion of the Erasmusbridge). On your way, you

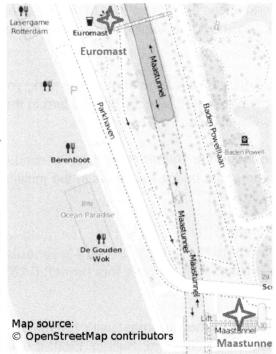

Map source:
© OpenStreetMap contributors

you will pass a huge, floating Chinese restaurant.

You already can see the ventilation building of the Maastunnel at the curve. The main entrance to the tunnel is a few meters further on the left.

The Maastunnel is a tunnel for cars, pedestrians, and bicycles. The tunnel runs under the **Nieuwe Maas**. Rotterdam started the building of the tunnel in 1937 and completed it during the German occupation. It was the first car tunnel in the Netherlands, too.

1944, the tunnel was to be blown up by the German army, but this did not work out. The exact reasons are unknown - one suspects that the Dutch resistance defused the explosions.

24

By F.Eveleens (Own work) [GFDL (http://www.gnu.org/copyleft/ fdl.html) or CC BY-SA 3.0 (http://creativecommons.org/licenses/by-sa/3.0)], via Wikimedia Commons

The foot and bicycle tunnels are completely separate from the car transport, so you are safe to walk. Worthy of note are the historic wooden stairs made of wood.

The tunnel has lost importance over the years, but is still an important link through Rotterdam, and is used by numerous pedestrians and cyclists in particular.

Please be careful: If you want to cross the Maastunnel, which will take about 30-45 minutes for the full way forth and back, please be sure to take the right floor:
The tracks for bicycles are right next to the escalators. It is dangerous to take this wrong way. Pedestrians have to go down one floor further.

When you finished your visit of the Maastunnel, it's time to take the way back to the starting point.

Leave the Maastunnel again on the side from which you have entered it and follow the watercourse towards Erasmusbridge (*Parkkade / Westerkade*).

After a few hundred meters you reach the *Veerhaven*: originally a real harbor part of Rotterdam, it is now used for yachts and historical sailing boats.

To get to the Erasmus Bridge is self-explanatory: If you have passed the Veerhaven, you enter the *Westerstraat* (trams are riding into this street, too). Keep going straight ahead until you reach the Erasmusbridge.

Enter the bridge: Congratulations, You have reached seen the most important sightseeing points of Rotterdam. I hope you enjoyed your journey trough Rotterdam.

But there is a lot more to do: See the original old steamship "SS Rotterdam", start a shopping tour or visit the beautiful Den Haag.

For some details, just read the next pages.

Attractions in Rotterdam

The Euromast
The Euromast is a 185-meter high tower and located in the city of Rotterdam. Opened in 1960, the tower had originally a height of 107 meters only. In the following years, some other new buildings were built even higher, so the „Space Tower" was added to the top in 1970.
Nowadays, you can visit the viewing platform and the restaurant in about 112 meters high. Further, a rotating elevator with glass panes (called Euroscoop) brings you to the height of 185 meters.
For the special kick, you can take the way down with a zip-line or a rope for 55 Euro, but you have to make an appointment earlier.

Entrance Fees 2017:
Adults: 9,75 Euro
Childen 4-11 years: 6,25 Euro
Seniors 65+ years: 8,75 Euro

SS Rotterdam
The former cruise ship SS Rotterdam is a real beauty: Built in 1959, it is the largest passenger ship that saw the light of day in the Netherlands. Operated until the year 2000, it is now a hotel and museum ship - and is waiting every day for you to visit

The ship has been extensively restored and still radiates the charm of the 50s and 60s. The Rotterdam itself is freely accessible, but it is really exciting with the different guided tours, which are offered daily: with Audioguides (small devices with headphones) they are also guided in several different languages by the ship. In addition, there are hourly guided tours of the old swimming pool, the machine rooms as well as the historical dining rooms and salons.

In addition to the guided tours, a public restaurant on the deck is freely accessible, other areas are accessible to hotel guests.

My opinion: If you are interested in ships, this exciting piece of history should not be missed.

Port of Rotterdam
First and foremost, Rotterdam is characterized by its huge harbor: it is by far the largest in Europe and about 40 kilometers long. In addition to container traffic, Also coal and petroleum.

In Rotterdam the individual port parts are sorted according to „house numbers" from 100 - 9900: This helps the truck drivers to pick-up and deliver their freight quickly.

Maasvlakte
There are numerous container terminals that are used by smaller inland vessels. For the huge container giants, some other terminals like the Maasvlakte were built.

The Maasvlakte is an artificial island, which was filled with sand from the sea. In 1973, the first part started to operate and allowed large ships with a high draft, a fast and comfortable mooring in Europe.

Since the forecasted container traffic will continue to rise, the construction of the so-called Maasvlakte 2 started in 2008: A complete island was filled with sea sand. The 3 billion (!) Euro project aims to absorb the increasing capacity utilization by at least 2030 - the capacity for container handling triples, using around 2,000 hectares for the port.

At the same time, a further 2,000 hectares are created as a nature conservation and recreation area. In addition, only 35% of all containers can be delivered and collected by truck from 2030 onwards, the remainder being loaded with more environmentally friendly means (inland waterway, train).

The port is huge – and unfortunately, there is almost no possibility to reach the port without a car. However, the operator of boat trips **Spido Tours** provides some harbor boat trips during the summer. See there website: https://www.spido.nl/en/

Zoo Rotterdam (Diergaarde Blijdorp)
The Diergaarde Blijdorp is a zoo in the middle of Rotterdam. It was founded in 1857 and now counts about 5800 animals in 600 different species on about 25 hectares.

The zoo is in continual modernization and according to the new standards. The visit of the zoo is highly recommended, but please note that it is huge and needs a lot of time to see everything.

Opening hours:
Summer: Daily from 8 am - 6 pm
Winter: Daily from 9 am – 7 pm

Entrance fees: adults 23, 00 Euro
Children (3-12) 18, 50 Euro
Children up to 2 years: Free of charge

How to get to:
By metro, line E (direction Den Haag) until station Blijdorp.
Then, follow the signs.

History: For the first time in 1855, two private individuals exhibited waterfowls and pheasants in the city center, which consisted of an association. In 1938, the zoo finally moved to its present location, as there was not enough space in the inner city and the land prices steadily increased.

In 1988, a master plan was issued to rebuild the zoo according to modern standards - this is still being implemented today.

Splash Tours
In Rotterdam, there are buses that also run into the water: These are the so-called amphibious vehicles. With Splash Tours you can experience a kind of a "different sightseeing tour" because the bus doesn't only show you the attractions by street, but also by water: That allows you a great view of the skyline of Rotterdam.
Also and especially for children, the ride into the water is a great experience.

Adults: €26,50
Children (up to 11 years): €18,00

Bus is departing from the Parkhaven (in the opposite from the Euromast), departing times are depending on the season, please check https://www.splashtours.nl/en/departure-times/

Kinderdijk

Kinderdijk is about 15 kilometers from Rotterdam and is known worldwide for its mills. These mills weren't built for grinding grain, but for pumping water. Today, most mills are driven electrically and are used for the tourism only. Many mills are now in private ownership and are inhabited, but one of the mills can still be visited from the inside and allows a great insight for the living in those times.

Since 1997, Kinderdijk is a UNESCO World Heritage site. From Rotterdam, you can reach Kinderdijk directly via the Erasmus Bridge with the waterbus.

Charges: €9,00 return, please check http://www.waterbus.nl/kinderdijk-en/ for departure times.

Mini World Rotterdam

Largest miniature world in Benelux with several different theming areas and an artificial change from day to night. Perfect for families with kids and rainy days.

Entrance fees:
Adults: 11, 50 Euro
Children under 11 years: 7, 50 Euro

Visiting hours:
During the summer opened every day, in the meantime sometimes closed on Mondays and Tuesdays.
Opened from 10.00 - 17.00 or from 12.00 to 17.00
Please check http://www.miniworldrotterdam.com/ENG_visit_visitinghours.htm for an exact schedule.

How to arrive from Amsterdam / How to get to Amsterdam

Many visitors of the Netherlands are arriving via Amsterdam Airport or are visiting the beautiful city of Amsterdam. Luckily, the Netherlands have a very well developed rail network which makes traveling easy.

Online schedule for the whole country:
Before you start your journey, you should always check the live schedule https://9292.nl/en# to avoid problems due to closed tracks or trains that are not driving.

Pricing:
The trip from Amsterdam Central

From Amsterdam, there are two direct train possibilities:

Direct Express train:
Rotterdam Central Station – Amsterdam Airport - Amsterdam Central Station
The train needs 42 minutes between Amsterdam CS. and Rotterdam CS.
A train is departing every 15 minutes.

Direct train:
Rotterdam Central Station – Amsterdam Central Station
The train needs 1 hour 15 minutes.
A train is departing every 15 minutes.

There are further possibilities for exchange in Leiden or Utrecht Centraal. Please check the website https://9292.nl/en# for more details or ask an employee at the local counter.I Station to Rotterdam Station (or vice versa) costs 15,20 Euro for an adult.

For the direct express train,
there is an additional of 2,40 Euro per person.

How to reach the city center by cruise ship

Are you visiting Rotterdam with a cruise ship?
My congratulations: When you are approaching the city of
Rotterdam, you will get a great view of the harbor terminals
and the skyline, which slowly appears on the horizon. Visiting
Rotterdam by cruise ship is really great!

But not only the journey to the city is an experience itself. Luckily, the cruise terminal is located in the city center and allows to
explore the attractions of the city easily by foot. But as there is
a metro station directly at the cruise terminal, you can make it
more comfortable and use the metro.

To reach the city center by foot, just walk over the Erasmusbridge and go straight for about 30 minutes.
You will reach the central point Beurs. To reach the town hall,
go straight, to reach Blaak (with Cube Houses, Market Hall,
and Laurens church) go right (about 10 minutes).
If you want to reach the city center by metro, take the station
Wilhelminaplein and use the line D (Direction: Rotterdam Centraal) or Line E (Direction: Den Haag Centraal).

How to use the public transport

Like all larger cities in the Netherlands, Rotterdam also has a well-developed public transport network: buses and trams also run through the city. The operator of railway lines and most buses is the company RET: *Rotterdamse Electric Tram*.

There is a great system nationwide, which makes it easy to travel quickly and without tariff confusion: The system is called *OV-Chipkaart*, which can be freely translated with "Public transport chip card"

Without a valid chip card, it is not possible to use buses, trams or metro trains. The underground trains are protected by electronic barriers that only can be opened with a chip card.

Regularly, these chip card is a great prepaid-system: You charge some money, check-in at your starting point and check-out at your destination. The system automatically calculates the fare and subtract the price from your balance.

In Rotterdam, you can buy a day ticket that is valid for the whole day. Luckily, this ticket is not that expensive and it already will be a good buy after the third trip.

It costs 7,50 Euro for the whole day.

To buy, just use one of the ticket machines that are located at every station. You can pay with cash (coins only!), your credit card (PIN-number required) or with the regular Maestro-card.

Public Transport: Metro lines

There are five metro lines in Rotterdam:
Line A, Line B, Line C, Line D and Line E.

Line A: Schiedam Centrum – Binnenhof
Line B: Schiedam Centrum – Nesselande
Line C: De Akkers – De Terp
Line D: De Akkers – Rotterdam Centraal
Line E: Slinge – Den Haag Centraal

When you are visiting Rotterdam as a tourist, only the metro stations in the city center will be interesting for you, with one exception: With line E, you can drive directly to The Hague, which is a totally different experience than visiting Rotterdam.

My recommendation: If you have seen anything in Rotterdam that is of interest to you, take the time and visit The Hague. It is very quick and easy to reach by metro.

The following are the most interesting metro stations for exploring the city of Rotterdam:

Delfshaven (lines A, B, C)
Historic port of Rotterdam,
Who have partially surrendered the Second World War

Dijkzigt (lines A, B, C)
The fastest way to the port museum as well as to Het Park, a large recreation area in the city center

Beurs (lines A, B, C, D, and E)
Central interchange point for all lines,
Good shopping possibilities in the city center

Rotterdam Central (lines D, E)
Newly built and modern main station

Blaak (lines A, B, C)
Market Hall, Kubushäuser, Laurenskerk, 2x weekly market, central place with many possibilities to eat and shop

Wilhelminian (lines D, E)
Here cruise ship, way to the „Kop van Zuid" (Hotel New York), great view of the water and the harbor

Rijnhaven (lines D, E)
From here about 20 minutes' walk to the
Museum ship „SS Rotterdam"

History of Rotterdam

When you take the time to visit Rotterdam, maybe you already visited other cities like Amsterdam, Groningen or Maastricht. Well, you will be surprised when you are arriving in Rotterdam: The city is completely different. There are almost no classical buildings or canals, but skyscrapers, unusual architecture and modern buildings. But what's the reason for that difference?

Rotterdam was founded in 1230 on the River Rotte. Rotterdam acquired the city rights around 1340, and then quickly developed into an influential trading city.

The ascent to the world port took place with the construction of the Nieuwe Waterweg. This is an excavation between the old dunes and the open sea.

The old port of Rotterdam was gradually dying, so construction began in 1866. Today, the Nieue Waterweg has a depth of around 11.60 meters and cannot be further deepened. Due to this, the new large port areas of Maasvlakte and Europoort has been created.

As a result of this development as well as the situation, Rotterdam grew steadily and also gained a strategic position in the world wars.

On May 14th, 1940, the inner city of Rotterdam was largely destroyed by a German air attack - about 80,000 people were homeless, about 800 died. Counter-attacks by the Allies as well as the destruction of the port facilities by the Germans against warfare did her the rest.

Since only isolated buildings have been preserved, a new beginning was made after the war: all pipes and drainage pipes were removed, streets were rebuilt, and landowners were expropriated for compensation to enable modern reconstruction. Ultimately, few buildings from the pre-war period have been preserved, including among others. The Laurenskerk, the Witte Huis, the Town Hall and the Hotel New York.

Today, Rotterdam is a very modern city and many renowned architects have settled down. In the last 20-25 years, a large skyscraper architecture has emerged in Rotterdam, with many buildings being unique and worth seeing.

Tips & Tricks

Rent a bike!
Dutch people are world champion in riding a bicycle: There are large bike trails and you can go by bike almost everywhere. It is really easy and highly recommended to rent a bike. There are several bike rentals in the city. I can recommend the rental at the central station Rotterdam Central. Just use the metro C, D, or E and drive until Rotterdam Central.

Cinema
Maybe the weather isn't good or you just want to relax: Go to the local cinema!
In the Netherlands, movies are not translated and can be watched (with Dutch subtitles) in English. The big cinema Pathé is located at the Schouwburgplein (near Rotterdam Central Station),
the smaller Cinerama is located near the central point Beurs

Food from the machine
it is looking awful, but is really tasty: Dutch people love to fry their food, and there are a lot of typical Dutch snacks you can buy at a vending machine.
You definitely should try:

The Kroket
A breaded and deep-fried croquette with meat and mashed potatoes is well-known and quite tasty. You should eat with mustard. The offshoots of these are the round bitterballen, which will be traditionally served in cafés, pubs, and bars. When you order a Bittergarnituur, you will get Bitterballen and a beer.
Tip: Only in the Dutch McDonalds-Restaurants is the „McKroket" available. It's a round Kroket, served in a burger ban.

Bamischijf
Is a breaded Bami: Noodles, vegetables, rare meat, and seasoning are pressed, breaded and finally fried.

Kaassoufflé
Melted cheese, breaded and fried.

Chocomel
Ready to drink- cocoa, served both warm and cold.

Frikandel
A sausage-like snack consisting of finely chopped beef, pork and poultry meat.

Joppiesaus
Sweet sauce for fries. It has a (not too strong) flavor of curry.

Poffertjes
Probably THE most famous specialty of the Dutch:
Small, round, baked pancakes. They are served with molten butter and powdered sugar, but in the Netherlands usually with sugar beet syrup (***Stroop***).

Vla
A classic pudding, but thin and ready to drink. It is available in various flavors: Chocolate, vanilla, strawberry, caramel… There are also some unusual sorts like ***Apple Cinnamon***.

Buy food in the Supermarket
The largest supermarket chain in the Netherlands is Albert Heijn. You will find a market often and can buy some snacks or drinks for the day. There are often some great special offers ("Buy one, get one free"), too.card. Watch out for the word PIN-KASSA.

Free information service

My free service for you:
You have a further question, a problem or a special request?
Send me a short mail to

info@rotterdamguide.net

and I will help you as soon as possible.

Further, I would be glad to receive your feedback:
I want that all visitors can enjoy their stay in Rotterdam, and your feedback helps me to improve my book for the future.

Impressum

Explore Rotterdam
Stephan Goedecke
Wacholderweg 8a
21244 Buchholz i.d.N.– Germany
info@rotterdamguide.net

Printed in Great Britain
by Amazon

42248945R00030